THE
SOCIAL MEDIA
PLAYBOOK
FOR COACHES AND
ADMINISTRATORS

JAY IZSO
The Internet Doctor®

Published by InterAction Press
Copyright © 2018 by Jay Izso

FIRST EDITION

InterAction Press
7300 Six Fork Road
Raleigh, NC 27615
www.interaction-press.com

Cover & Interior Design:
GKS Creative, www.gkscreative.com

Library of Congress Case Number 1-6858293041

ISBN: 978-0-9915136-8-0 (paperback)
ISBN: 978-0-9915136-9-7 (e-book)

For media or booking inquiries, please contact:

STRATEGIES Public Relations
P.O. Box 178122
San Diego, CA 92177
858-467-1978
jkuritz@strategiespr.com

PRINTED IN THE UNITED STATES OF AMERICA ON ACID-FREE PAPER.

This book is dedicated to the athletic coaches and administrators. For those of us who were student athletes, you made a larger impact on us young women and men than any professor. You actually came to know us, not as another person sitting at a desk . . . but for years of our lives you saw us nearly every day. You invested your time in us. You knew our darkest secrets and kept them to yourselves. You knew our strengths and our weaknesses. You knew our families. You knew us, in reality, better than we knew ourselves. You became our family for sometimes four or five years. As a matter of fact we spent more time with you during that time than any other group of people. We often put you in difficult positions, and yet you found away to demonstrate mercy, withholding the punishment we surely deserved.

We probably will forget to tell you on the way out the door as we embark on some sort of professional career . . .

THANK YOU!

You made a difference in our lives!

TABLE OF CONTENTS

INTRODUCTION

What can I say to you as coaches and administrators about social media that you probably have not already heard and thought of? How about social media is, in reality, a great thing for your college or university. Probably not your first thought. As a matter of fact, you are probably thinking something like, "Jay, you have no idea what type of damage control we are in when it comes to social media, and you say it is a great thing?" Yes, I did. And I stand by it.

First, let me just say as a former student athlete and someone who was paid from athletic department budgets, I understand how sensitive you are to all sorts of scrutiny—whether that scrutiny is from the national athletic governing bodies, parents, other schools, professors, non-athletic administration, and let us not forget the media. They all seem to want to find something that will take you down or discredit you or your hard work. There is no rest for you coaches and administrators. You are on call twenty-four hours, seven days a week. If one athlete gets in an accident, drinks and drives, is caught in a place they should not have been, gets pregnant, gets charged with assault, or doesn't pay a bill in a restaurant, it is front page headlines. Add to that social media. I understand that your first reaction is "Yes, Jay, add social media and you can understand why it is a problem." That is the reflex; and the reflex is, in and of itself, a problem.

Social media is a tough subject—a hot potato—in athletic departments. No matter who I talk to in athletic administration (all off the record I might add, because no one, and I mean no one, would allow me to talk to them on the record about social media), when I bring up the subject of social media you would think I had just mentioned the word "cancer." All of a sudden the room gets quiet. No one knows exactly what to say. Everyone in athletics keeps their mouths tightly closed. I experienced this when trying to do interviews for this book. Every college or university I reached out to refused to speak with me on the subject. Fear is powerful. When otherwise rational, intelligent, well-meaning people refuse to speak about a common subject, I know at the very heart of it is fear. We need to change that.

By not addressing the problem appropriately, rationally, and positively we have created a bigger problem. Rather than controlling the medium of social media, as coaches and administrators we have allowed social media to control us. That is not the way it is supposed to be! When I see the amount of fear being displayed by athletic departments it is no surprise that many of them have banned social media in season, or forced students to shut down their accounts by threatening them with loss of scholarships. Fear is no way to live. When we experience fear as human beings, we become reflexive, react emotionally (mostly anger), and attempt to control the environment. Of all the people who should fight this tendency, athletic department coaches and administrators are at the top of the list. All of you work in a world based on unpredictability of opponents, unpredictable game situations, and having to make adjustments on the fly to put your people in the best possible position for success. Social media should not be any different in your day-to-day strategy and plan.

The biggest mistake that any company can make that will inhibit their success is "managing to an exception." Oh it sounds good, because it appears to be the safest course of action. But the fact is, when you manage to the exception you punish the majority. It is the wrong message. As human beings and administrators we tend to punish or restrict first. It is the easiest thing to do. We operate from a world of "don't do this" and "don't do that" and add the clincher "or else." Who wants to live in that world? Do you? I certainly don't. It is probably why I left the athletic department and college and university as a career, because we were always managing to an exception, punishing the innocent for the problem of one person, and then rationalizing it as if it were "the right thing to do." Why?

It really wasn't for the student athlete. It was simply to keep us out of headlines and make our own job easier. We penalized the vast majority of really great kids for the mistakes of one or a few. Doing this is wrong, and it sends the wrong message. Here we are, supposedly intelligent people, who are considered leaders, coaches, executives, and administrators, and we cannot handle the pressure. We worry about potential pain. We would rather take punitive and restrictive actions on the innocent, believing somehow—or perhaps convincing ourselves—that "it was for their own good" or "they will get over it." Do they? Or did they just learn over the course of their time in our orbit that people in power can restrict or punish the innocent without retribution?

The fact is social media is neither good nor bad. Rather, it is a communication tool. Period. Snapchat, Instagram, Twitter, Facebook, etc. They did not set out to make the world a bad place. They have no desire to hurt your athletic department. They simply provided a medium by which people can communicate instantly everything in their lives.

And yes I mean everything. Every thought, every place, every movement, every event, everything they eat, drink, wear or don't wear ... everything. That doesn't make these places evil. It simply means that people need to be coached on how to use these platforms in a way that is beneficial to themselves, their families, and their place of business (in this case their college or university). We spend a great deal of time and money coaching young people's bodies to perform a desired behavior in the heat of competition. If we spent just a little time understanding how to use these platforms in a way that would benefit your program and university, you could achieve the same success with social media platforms.

Once your young people know that you are a proponent of these social platforms and are willing to coach them to be good at it, to use the platforms in ways that will enhance their online profiles, that it will help them not just right now while they are student athletes but will help later to begin their professional careers, they will get on board. And when prospective athletes see how your institution is utilizing social media for the benefit of your athletes, recruiting becomes easier.

After years researching users on these different platforms, I am convinced that the different social media platforms are nothing more than cultures. They each have their own language and their own unwritten rules, norms, and expectations. Engaging on them at first is, in fact, no different than going to a foreign land where you do not know the language or the cultural norms and expectations. We would not, for instance, try to sell a hamburger in India. If, in ignorance, we did so, it would not make the culture the problem, it would simply mean that we lacked education and training about that culture necessary to being successful in the culture. Social media is not the problem. These are great cultures that can add value to your student athlete as well as your college or university. The bigger issue is coaching these young minds on how to appropriately interact with the culture to set them up for future success.

The key is to be the coach that you are. You would never coach from the aspect of "don't do this" or "don't do that." Taking a page from how we coach on the field, we need to coach them on what they should do. How and why these cultures can add to their success as professionals in the future. This book has been written to help you further understand these cultures and to give you practical useful tools to help your student athlete interact within these cultures in a way that can make you both more successful. Psychology has demonstrated that punishment is the easiest consequence to apply. However, we also know that punishment paradigms are not effective when it comes to learning. Ultimately, you as a coach and administrator are about helping these young people learn lessons today that will positively affect them in their future. We know that if we can apply these methods in a positive manner the probability of learning dramatically increases.

I am asking you to change your mindset when it comes to these platforms/cultures. I am asking you to use this book to further discover ways that you can use these cultures to enhance your brand as an institution, to coach these young people how to use them so they will enhance their ability to find their next career position. I know what I am asking is not going to be easy. But as we all know, anything worth doing comes with some struggle, a trial or two, and some pain. I am asking you to not react. I am asking you to be open. Think differently. You have been blessed to be in a position as a leader and educator. There is a reason you are where you are, and that is to make a positive difference in the lives of young people. Social media is just one more place in today's world where you can both lead and educate—and ultimately coach. Be that person that your young people can look to as a mentor. I know you can, I know you will.

Be inspired!

Jay Izso, the Internet Doctor®

1

SOCIAL MEDIA 101

Who would have thought even ten years ago that it would be necessary to have a conversation about online communication and college athletics? Who could have predicted that social media would become the most popular form of sports-related communication and a global news–breaking forum? The world of college athletics has changed, hasn't it? As complicated as the NCAA compliance rules can be on their own, social media certainly compounds these challenges exponentially as social media changes how interactions like recruiting are orchestrated and the rules of what you can and cannot do on social media change.

The truth is, we probably should have seen social media coming. The Internet, instant messaging, chat rooms, and Skype have been around for years. It makes sense that somehow people would combine them to create a real-time visual communication exchange. Add to that the technological leaps that have made the mobile phone smart: smartphones do more than your desktop computer did ten years ago and can be carried in your hand! Some of you are better adjusted to this new milieu than others. Whatever your level of technological savvy, there's room to learn. I've written this book for all of you coaches and administrators navigating this brave new world to address social media as it applies to the college athletics scene. What you read here is not going to be like what you hear from everyone else.

A number of books have already been published about social media. I have written this book with college coaches and administrators in mind. I played college football and have written extensively about the psychology of social media and how people use it and perceive it. I understand both how social media can work for people in positive ways but also how people can use it in ways that reflect poorly on them. I have interviewed college coaches, administrators, and athletes, and one theme consistently arose: uncertainty surrounds social media, and most people don't know what exactly they should do or not do when using it.

The primary reason I wrote the book was that I kept hearing coaches and administrators default to a "don't do" strategy. They felt it was easier to tell student athletes not to post than it was to help them understand how they could use social media safely and with an eye toward laying the groundwork for future career opportunities. I found this interesting, because great coaches never coach their players by simply telling them "don't do that." No, great coaches not only correct inappropriate behavior but provide strategies to achieve success. I know you are well educated in coaching and athletics. My goal here is to give you a deeper understanding of social media and provide you with ideas and suggestions that you can use to truly coach your student athletes to be more successful on social media and reduce your worry about your athletes' use of social media.

Some people think social media is nonsense, worthless, useless, ridiculous, and a waste of time. Well, consider that Facebook by itself is closing in on 2 billion people. And consider that there are people using multiple platforms that number is growing and is destined to continue. Those numbers alone gives it value. Social media also provides insight into the way that people's minds work and what their social needs are. With that information in hand, it is possible to figure out how a person can most effectively connect to other people on social media and build a healthy reputation there.

I have been researching, studying, and using social media from its inception. Do you remember MySpace? I think I still have a MySpace account floating around cyberspace somewhere. Because of my background in psychology, however, social media has never been just some fun thing to do. It became my passion to understand how people use it, why they are motivated to use it, how they respond to different types of posts, how each platform is actually a separate culture, and the psychology behind all of it. Once my study and analysis of social media usage yielded answers to my questions, I developed an even greater drive to help other people understand not just the nuts and bolts of the technology of social media but also how users are acting and interacting on each platform. Ultimately, I want to enable people (like you!) to maximize the potential benefits of these platforms and, in so doing, provide tools that help others understand how to maximize social media's potential.

I call this study of social media and psychology *social mediology*—the study of social media that considers the psychological aspects of the user and the social psychological and cultural aspects of each platform. Most people know the basics of building a profile, adding pictures, and posting. Your student athletes do it from their phones almost intuitively. Although knowledge of the mechanics of using social media is helpful, that is not your biggest concern or problem. It is what student athletes post that you should be most concerned about, because what your student athletes post is what has the potential to get them into trouble. Understanding the technology will not help you with this problem. The psychology of why your student athletes are motivated to post what they do, how to change their online behavior, and how to improve the odds that the people reading their posts will come away with positive perceptions of your athletes are what I want you to understand. Here, I will provide you with strategies you can use to teach these young women and men how to be better on social media than they are right now.

WHAT IS SOCIAL MEDIA?

There are myriad definitions of what social media is and is not. I subscribe to a simple definition: social media is any online platform where people can post words, pictures, or videos that have the potential to be viewed by anyone in real time.

Let's consider those two words separately: *social* and *media*. The social aspects of social media allow users to connect with others and exchange thoughts and ideas. The social dimension of social media is very attractive to the people who use it, because humans desire interaction with their fellow humans. Social media is fun, enables communication, and draws people in by fulfilling the universal human need for

connection. Quite frankly, connectivity is the most significant aspect of social media. It allows people to stay in touch,
deepen passing relationships into friendships, share good
news, and ask for support when it is needed.

Then there is the *media* portion of social media. This is
the part that you, as a coach or an administrator, need to
pay the most attention to. It is also the piece that your student athlete understands the least. It has the potential to
be the more dangerous aspect of social media. Although
being social is all well and good, when the things that
people post cross a line, often one of taste or decency, the
media part takes over. A post that inspires a reaction in
viewers can go viral in hurry. Whether or not a post goes
viral, once it is posted, even if the original poster deletes
it, it can never truly be erased. Take, for instance, a tweet
by Cardale Jones, from when he was a quarterback at Ohio
State University.

Please note that this tweet was posted in 2012. Once he realized the post was problematic, Jones deleted this post and shut down his account. Yet, even now, if you type "Cardale Jones tweet" in Google, this is the first thing that pops up on the search results. Not only is the tweet not gone, it will live on in infamy! This is just one example of the power of the media aspect of social media. One wrong post can go viral on its own or be picked up by the news media (usually both) and, in minutes, millions of people are reading it. Your young athletes do not understand this danger or its consequences. They don't even think about the possibility that one social media mistake can be amplified in such a way, much less be immortalized and inescapable. If they do, they don't think that something like this can happen to them. You can give them all of the media training in the world, but if they do not have social media training, this will continue to happen.

Your athletes who use social media do understand one part of the media aspect of social media: they know that what they say can get them attention. Many of them like that attention, and some of them like it tremendously. Further, you and they will find that a small amount of attention can lead to more attention. This is quite often why student athletes push the envelope of propriety with their posts. They are intentionally pushing the limits to get a reaction, but they are not posting material with the goal of harming themselves or their athletic program. They simply do not connect the dots when it comes to what they say and the consequences that can result. When I talk to college-age students, they give me the same rhetoric: "Well, I have freedom of speech, I can say what I want." My response is very simple: "Yes, you do have freedom of speech, but you do not have freedom from consequences. The government does not protect you on social media."

This is where young athletes often stumble when it comes to social media. A troubling number firmly believe that a part of "freedom of speech" is "freedom from consequences." The challenge for you and me is to get them to understand that there is no such thing as freedom from consequences. Further, when it comes to social media platforms, even the initial premise of "freedom of speech" is not guaranteed. Because social media platforms are privately owned, the owners of these platforms have the right to delete anything they want (I say a bit more on this topic in chapter 3, under myth 6).

Every national media outlet has a social media presence. This means that not only are writers and journalists reporting the news, they are searching for news. An easy place to look for news that people will read is athletics: professional; college; high school; Divisions 1, 2, and 3; NAIA; women's sports; men's sports—it doesn't matter. Athletics is—please excuse the expression—a wide-open field in which reporters can find news. This is a fine situation when the news about your program is good. However, reporters are always looking for stories that generate reader reaction; unfortunately, negative stories fit this bill, especially when it comes to social media sentiment. If you can minimize the number of times your athletes draw attention to your school and athletic program with foolish or negative posts, so much the better.

The national news media is not the only entity that is interested in the negative things that student athletes say or do. Social media is home to a whole legion of wannabe reporters itching for their chance to share breaking news first. Thanks to social media, today everyone thinks they are part of the news media. Plenty of people would be happy to find a little juicy nugget from some athlete's social media feed that they can post on their rarely read blog to attract eyes, clicks, and perhaps a bit of credit for their discovery.

Here is the real danger of athletes and social media: national news people have real jobs, so they are busy investigating any number of stories. Members of the general public are the ones who typically bring social media posts to the attention of the ESPNs of the world, elevating a social media gaffe to the level of a SportsCenter story. Here is where your young athletes and even coaches are naïve regarding the media aspect of social media: they think that all of the people who follow them, like them, and retweet them are supporters. However, to be savvy in this social media world, you have to assume that among your followers are people who are willing to exploit, expose, or pillory an athlete who posts something even marginally inappropriate or questionable. Blame the news media all you want, but the general public often feeds stories to the news media. Your athletes need to understand that their followers and friends do not always have their best interest at heart. In a heartbeat, some predators will trade their social media following and friendship just so they can feel as if they are "in the know" and can be the first ones to break the story. The sacrifice is worth it to them.

I am not trying to be negative about social media. When used correctly and wisely, social media has many benefits. Because of both the social and the media aspects of social media, an athlete, coach, or school can build a positive brand that others want to be a part of. True, using social media the right way takes time and commitment, because being positive is something that must be done regularly to attract attention and be recognized. Conversely, one undiplomatic, inappropriate tweet that gets retweeted to the general public can knock an athlete, a school, and their brands back several steps. However, if you use it in the right way, social media can help you build some amazing social capital that can go a long way with fans, recruits, and even future employers. To achieve all of this, you need to understand the platforms that your athletes are going to use, how people use them, and the psychology behind them.

2

THE PLATFORMS

In my book *Got Social Mediology? Using Psychology to Master Social Media for Your Business without Spending a Dime*, I wrote about how the different social media platforms are really cultures, like foreign countries with their own languages, unwritten rules, norms, and expectations. Understand that it wasn't the owners of these platforms who created these cultures: the cultures were brought into being by the users themselves. This is why when you or your athletes violate the unwritten rules, norms, or expectations of a platform, negative consequences result.

I am not going to teach you how to post on Facebook or explain the technology behind Snapchat. If you don't already know how to use them, there are plenty of sources out there that can teach you the basics. Rather, in what follows, I briefly talk about each platform as a culture while noting a few interesting things about the psychology of the people on these platforms and the appeal and the dangers of each platform for your athlete.

FACEBOOK

Facebook is a casual, relaxing, family-and-friend-centered culture. After all, people connected with each other on this platform are called—wait for it—friends. It is worth noting here that the name given to the connections people make on different social media platforms will always be a cultural cue for that platform. Next, it is important to note that although Facebook posts can consist entirely of text, the most popular posts are photos and videos. You can even run live video on Facebook! I am sure more and more athletes will take advantage of the live video feeds to enhance their brands or simply garner more attention.

Facebook Revival: Facebook Live

Perhaps you are of the mind that Facebook is old school. Many student athletes and young people have said in the past that they only use it to stay in touch with their families. However, we are beginning to see a bit of a shift back to Facebook use, even for the younger generation, thanks to Facebook Live. Facebook Live is a new addition to Facebook that allows people to stream a live broadcast from their Facebook profile. People can now pick up their smartphones, click on the Facebook Live button, and immediately start streaming anything they want. What is more, they can receive live commentary while they are broadcasting. Once the broadcast is over, people can continue to comment, like, or share the broadcast.

This feature has created a new interest in Facebook for the younger users who may have been moving away from Facebook. It is important that you, as coaches and administrators, not only understand Facebook Live but also learn to use it so that you can take advantage of it. Facebook Live has become increasingly popular as it has rolled out to Facebook users. As with any video, of course, there are dangers, such as content than contains language, sexual content, alcohol and drug use etc., but because it is live streaming, there are also some great opportunities to promote your athletics program, shine a spotlight on your athletes, and expand your brand's positive image. If you have not started using Facebook Live, take some time to investigate it and consider how you might work it into your school's branding strategy.

A recent survey revealed that 97 percent of student athletes have a Facebook account.[1] However, the majority of them are using it less than they did a year ago, and some are not using their account at all, although they maintain it. Many younger adults do not use Facebook because it is the one social media platform that their parents and grandparents are likely using. Therefore, your athletes may glance at their accounts, but only to stay aware of what's going on with their families. However, even though your student athletes may not be actively using Facebook, it is still the most used platform in every age group. With over 1.5 billion users, it is a beast! And despite what some people think, it is still growing.

My research indicates that normally, athletes get in less trouble on Facebook than they do on other platforms. One study suggests that athletes understand the Facebook culture pretty well, and, because family is there, most of them are pretty careful about what they post. However, there are times when people will get carried away in a Facebook discussion focused on some hot topic, like the local rival team, and they say something in a crude way or swear in reference to the rival team's players, coaches, or school. At that point, what we used to call "bulletin board material" is now digital board material. I admit, this kind of indiscretion is rare, but it occasionally happens. Look, whatever your opinion is of Facebook and even if your student athletes say it is dead or they do not use it, do not neglect it. It is the single largest social media platform on the planet and is still growing. Although it may not be used daily by your student athletes, it still could be the source of both good and harm for you and your student athlete.

TWITTER

Twitter culture is about followers, plain and simple. You could argue that it represents a popularity contest. For athletes and coaches, it is the most commonly used platform and seems to work best for those who have some semblance of fame or celebrity status. Things happen quickly on Twitter. It is a great way to keep up with other coaches, current athletes, future recruits, media, and others. Your athletes will be following the sports media, and the sports reporters often return the favor by following the athletes.

Much of the popularity of Twitter for athletes is for three reasons. First, it is heavily used by the media, which includes the sports media, and is a place where young athletes can keep with the latest sports news, scores, and updates about other athletes. This leads to the second reason: it is where many of their sports heroes talk about their lives, their sport, and a multitude of issues. In many instances, student athletes follow their heroes and, in turn, because they too are considered athletes, they get followed back. Third, it is popular for athletes because it is the fastest way of gaining a significant number of followers without having to follow, friend, or reach out to others. Student athletes get attention quite quickly once they are on Twitter; the followers simply come because they are athletes. Why does this happen? Credit a psychological phenomenon known as *parasocial contact*. Parasocial contact, simply put, is when people follow athletes and celebrities because they believe that following famous people creates a connection with them. The followers may even feel like they are personally connected to or part of the entourage of the athlete or celebrity, despite the fact that the athlete or celebrity may not even know most of their followers in real life.

In addition to the media and groupies, a third group of people on Twitter will interact with you and your athletes. This group is not large in number, but its members do exist, and they specialize in catching attention. They are known as *trolls*, *shamers*, and *flamers*, and they follow an athlete or coach with the intention of baiting that person into saying something inappropriate, waiting for an athletic celebrity to say one wrong thing so that they can make a snide remark, shaming the celebrity publicly, or engaging the person they are following in an argument, again with the purpose of getting the celebrity to say something he or she should not.

As beneficial as Twitter can be for you and your athletes, it is also one of the most dangerous cultural platforms, and it is certainly the platform where the greatest number of athletes and coaches get in trouble. Why? Because people often do not think before they tweet. Twitter can be the fastest way to lose your job or the method by which an athlete can lose a scholarship in 140 or fewer characters.

There was a time when coaches and athletes could say something crass in an interview, but the reporter, who often would travel with the team, would serve as a diplomatic interpreter with a bit of a censor thrown in for good measure and good copy. However, a new phenomenon is emerging when it comes to social media. The reporter, who used to act as a filter, has been removed from the process. Now, when the coach or athlete essentially self-publishes on social media, thoughts originate in that person's mental and emotional state and travel to his or her fingers with no filter in between. You would think that at some point in the process we would be able to stop or otherwise find just a few seconds to reflect before our fingers hit *enter*. However, we do not. I believe there are two reasons for this lack of control.

First, the phone, the tablet, the laptop, and the desktop act as a protective barrier between us and an audience. We have a sense of autonomy when we are posting on our own, like our thoughts are going into a diary rather than online for all to see. At that moment, others do not exist. Plus, by using our fingers to tap out a message on our device, things that we would never say out loud somehow become OK to express. It is as if we do not believe that what we type really means what it would if we said it. You are sharing your thoughts with a device devoid of any human emotion or reaction. You forget that the device is going to broadcast those thoughts to anyone who cares to read them.

This leads me to my second reason why we automatically type what is in our head, and that is a lack of social cues.

When we are at some social engagement or around people we do not know well, we rely on social cues to determine what to say or, more important, what not to say. These social cues provide us with immediate feedback regarding what topics are safe for us to talk about and which ones we should avoid, as well as the type of language we can use or should avoid. On Twitter (and all social media, for that matter), we often do not have these cues. What is worse, the cues that we do get come after we post, not before. This is perhaps the biggest reason why people are so willing to say anything on Twitter.

To make things worse, you only get 140 characters in which to express yourself, which is not much. It is hard to convey a complete and nuanced thought, much less a line of reasoning, in such a brief space. These 140 characters can become even more cryptic when one adds emojis (those smiley faces and other images that replace words). With those meager tools, how much trouble can one get into? In the sports world, as we have seen and will continue to see, plenty.

You could take Coach Nick Saban's approach and not even have a Twitter account. However, I do not think that can work for most coaches. Recruiting is about knowing and marketing to your demographic. Athletes love Twitter. They are looking for your interaction. A coach savvy enough to use this platform in the right way can have a tremendous advantage in the recruiting battle.

INSTAGRAM

You may not be aware of this, but Instagram is the second largest social media platform out there today. Did you know that Facebook owns Instagram? This is why people will often post to both simultaneously, and it is also another reason why Facebook may still be relevant with younger athletes. Instagram is a smartphone-only picture- and video-sharing platform that has some features in common with Twitter and Facebook. It is similar to Facebook in that you can post pictures and videos and people can make comments on them. It is similar to Twitter in that it is about having followers. The difference is that someone can follow you on Instagram but, depending on your privacy control settings, unless you approve them to follow you, they cannot see what you post.

You may think that all social media is pretty narcissistic; however, Instagram takes the naval gazing to another level. As an Instagram user, you are forced to post a picture or video, unlike on Facebook or Twitter, where you have the option of posting text-only messages. Hence, selfies (photos one takes of oneself) abound on Instagram. Also, on Instagram, like on Facebook, people who you have approved to follow you can comment on your photo or video; however, unlike on Facebook, you cannot like their comments, you can only reply to them. Further, you are limited to sharing posts only with another person whom you follow. This means that an Instagram post has the potential to make the leap from your feed into the world, perhaps even go viral, but it takes some effort to get it out there.

Again, this is a platform that is growing in popularity with student athletes. Their biggest downfall is believing that on Instagram they have more freedom to do things than they may have on Twitter. Although the privacy controls are a bit more restrictive, should your athlete even employ them, they are still not foolproof. Athletes have created trouble for themselves by posting inappropriate pictures and videos on Instagram, which subsequently got shared with the wrong person, who then had the ammunition to exploit the athlete or otherwise make the athlete's life difficult.

For you as a coach, keep in mind that this is where your demographic is, so do yourself a favor: get an account going and pay attention to those recruits, provided they allow you to follow them and see their pictures.

SNAPCHAT

Snapchat is one of the newer, growing platforms on the block that student athletes and the younger generation just love. Snapchat, like Instagram, is a smartphone-only sharing application. Like Twitter and Instagram, to be successful on it, a Snapchat user has to have followers. These followers must be approved by the user—in this case, the student athlete. The appeal to the young, when it comes to Snapchat, is that you can take a picture or short (up to a ten-second-long) video and post it, and it disappears after it has been seen. Well, that's what Snapchat users believe, anyway. In reality, that is not true. This is where coaches, family, and even most users misunderstand the platform.

Although it is true that Snapchat videos and photos disappear from the viewer's feed after a period of time, and it is also true that Snapchat notifies the user if someone takes a screenshot of the picture or video he or she has posted, third-party applications can save the picture or video permanently on the viewer's phone and your athlete will never know. Snapchat has done a decent job of limiting the functionality of these third-party apps, but new ones pop up regularly. Another thing people are doing to capture the photo or video is using another phone to take a video or picture of the phone that is displaying Snapchat. There is no way anyone would know that this has been done until a rerecorded photo or video showed up on another social media site or Snapchat feed. Yes, this is the extent to which people are willing to go to catch people in a compromising moment.

By the way, let's be honest: even if you are notified that someone has taken a screenshot of a compromising picture or video you have posted, it is too late for you to do anything about it. You can remove the offender from your follower list, but the picture or video is already on that person's phone or computer, where it waits for that person to decide when the moment is right to unleash it on the world. This is a situation in which knowing what defensive play you should deploy will become important (see chapter 10 for strategies).

You are probably already seeing the potential problems that can arise when the users of this platform believe their *snaps* (the term Snapchat uses for posted pictures or videos) are going to permanently disappear, leaving no evidence. Any thoughts on what types of inappropriate things these young folks post? You guessed it: snaps of partying, drinking, smoking marijuana, and, yes, nudity. In regard to this last item, Snapchat has said that it is limiting such posts and that there is very little nudity or pornography on Snapchat. Yet there are so many pornography stars and strippers on Snapchat it is difficult to avoid them. In other words, don't count on Snapchat to catch and take down your athlete's one indiscreet photo.

Of all of the platforms where student athletes have admitted to posting something inappropriate—that is, material that includes profanity, racial content, drugs, alcohol, violence, or nudity—Snapchat ranks the highest. According to the 2016 Fieldhouse Media study, 45 percent of survey respondents admitted to posting something inappropriate on it.[2] I believe the real number, which would include those who have posted something inappropriate but have not admitted it, is even higher. Just as a comparison, the social media platform with the second highest percentage of survey respondents admitting to inappropriate posts is Twitter, with 26 percent. These statistics may surprise you because of the popularity of Twitter with athletes. However, Snapchat has more daily users than Twitter. Hence, student athletes are apt to post more frequently on Snapchat than on Twitter.

For now, Snapchat is a platform that you as a coach may or may not use or even consider using. Because the culture is based so much on privacy, my guess is that your student athletes probably are not going to let you into their Snapchat follower circles for you to get a candid look at what they do anyway. Some coaches and athletic departments from a variety of sports have adopted Snapchat, knowing that the platform is one many young people visit daily. Also, they realize that it is a potential recruiting tool. You will have to make the decision about participation for yourself. Remember that if you're on Snapchat, you need followers. What that means is that you may have to follow others first if you want to be followed. Regardless of your choice, it is important to emphasize to your athletes who do use it that you know how it works; help them understand that Snapchat is not as private as they think and that there are ways for people to save their snaps without their knowledge. It only takes one person sharing the wrong snap to ruin a young woman or young man's entire athletic career.

OTHER PLATFORMS

Other social media platforms are also available, such as Pinterest, LinkedIn, Google+, and Tumblr. However, these platforms are not used very often by student athletes and, thankfully, they represent one (or even four) fewer thing to concern yourself with.

CONCLUSION

You need to know which social media platforms your athletes are using: how they work, what your student athletes do on them, and both the positive and the negative aspects of each one. Look, these platforms offer some great benefits for both your student athletes and you. If you do well on these platforms, they can even help you with recruiting. If a student athlete uses these platforms in a positive way, it can build your program's brand as well as your athlete's. This is why understanding how people use a particular social media platform, what their motivations are for using it, and the psychology of social media viewers on that platform can tremendously benefit you and your program.

3

SIX MYTHS ABOUT ATHLETES AND SOCIAL MEDIA

Myths typically start as rumors. However, let people believe a rumor long enough and it will come to be accepted as fact. I have identified six myths regarding athletes on social media, and a few apply to coaches, too. Bust these myths and you will have a clearer, more useful understanding of social media and how to keep your athletes and your program on a positive track.

MYTH 1: STUDENT ATHLETES CAN SAY WHAT THEY WANT BECAUSE THEY ARE YOUNG

Just because someone is young doesn't mean that that person can say and do whatever he or she wants on social media and be forgiven. People might be kind enough to take an offender's youth into consideration, but the poster will likely have the bad post popping up at inopportune times for the rest of his or her career. Take Kris Boyd, a freshman defensive back at the University of Texas. During one game, Texas was getting blown out by Texas Christian University. By halftime, the game was virtually over. Boyd went to his

locker at halftime and grabbed his phone to check on his social media mentions. As he looked at Twitter, he saw he was
mentioned in the following tweets:

Some players, fans, coaches, and administrators are probably
saying, "What in the heck is this guy doing checking his phone
at halftime?" It's a great question that only Boyd can answer.
However, that was not Boyd's downfall. His problem was that
he decided to retweet both of these to all of his followers. Some
of you may be thinking or saying, "No big deal." You would be
wrong. The second tweet is from a Texas A&M fan.

"What's the problem?" you may ask. Well, Boyd is getting
an athletic scholarship from the University of Texas. He
signed a letter committing to the University of Texas, and
the university has certain expectations regarding his con-
duct as a result of his signature. In one retweet—not even
adding a word of his own, simply by clicking—Boyd posted
a message readable by everyone in the world that made him
look like he was considering transferring. That was probably
not his intent, but the damage was done. He subsequently
apologized, but it didn't matter. The major media outlets ate

it up! Does Boyd really want to be at the University of Texas? What does this say about University of Texas football players? Are they angry with the coach? The administrators? Mad about the game? Is he leaving? What the heck is going on at the University of Texas that they cannot keep their athletes from embarrassing their institution? The questions flew fast and furious.

It does not matter how young an athlete is when making such a misstep, because, as Boyd will soon find out, memories for mistakes are long. As his career advances, he is likely to find that there will always be extra questions and scrutiny over everything he ever says or does on social media. What he thought was funny enough to share now puts him in a position where he is forever identified as the disloyal University of Texas halftime retweeter.

MYTH 2: PEOPLE ONLY CARE ABOUT DIVISION 1 ATHLETES AND COACHES; THEY DON'T CARE ABOUT DIVISION 2, DIVISION 3, OR SMALLER SCHOOLS

When one is an athlete or coach, regardless of the level of play, one is under the microscope. Although it's more natural to you to think of your athletes and coaches as having peers only at your level of play, much of the public lumps all student athletes and their coaches together under the banner of "people involved in college sports." Remember how Aunt Maude asks you every Thanksgiving when the men's basketball team you coach will ever play at her alma mater, a tiny women's college tucked into the hillside of a state nowhere near your conference? Assume that most people are like Aunt Maude.

Unfortunately, this means that the on- and offline behavior of any number of athletes and coaches at all levels of the game is going to reflect on you, whether you like it or not. You can have 10,000 coaches and athletes from all levels of play say and do the right thing in real life and on social media, and no one cares. Yet when an assistant coach from a small school posts something inappropriate or a football player from a Big Ten school gets drunk and assaults someone and brags about it on Facebook, you and your people are going to be getting the side-eye from the community, a few new rules from the dean, and a talking to by the director of the college athletic department.

MYTH 3: NO ONE CARES ABOUT SPORTS OTHER THAN FOOTBALL AND BASKETBALL WHEN IT COMES TO SOCIAL MEDIA

Athletes belong to a very select group of people. It doesn't matter if they play football, volleyball, soccer, baseball, basketball, lacrosse, tennis, or underwater ping-pong. Your athletes represent all athletes, both past and present, regardless of your sport. When one athlete says something stupid on Twitter, it causes people to wonder if all athletes are that stupid. The same can be said for coaches.

MYTH 4: IF I TELL PEOPLE THAT MY ACCOUNT WAS HACKED OR SAY, "I WAS TAKEN OUT OF CONTEXT," PEOPLE WILL LEAVE IT ALONE

Oh, you or your athlete can say this, but the general public won't believe it, even if it is true. What is more, the news media will greet such excuses with a wink and nudge and make jokes about how naïve the person was who used this excuse to explain away his or her social media posting sins. Excuses are excuses. The public does not buy it, and you do not buy it. The best advice you can give your athlete is to take responsibility, and you need to model this behavior should you not take my advice and find yourself in social media hot water. Anyone who has done wrong on social media needs to apologize for a bad post, make amends where they can be made, and move on.

MYTH 5: SOCIAL MEDIA IS MY BUSINESS, NOT YOURS

Actually, social media is everyone's business—that's the social part. Your athlete posted it. People are looking for it. Some are friends and fans who want updates from their favorite players. Others have not-so-nice intentions. They are the predators ready to pounce. They want to do whatever they can to discredit your player not only as an athlete but also as a person. Your athlete may say and even think that his or her social media is his or her business, but the fact is, whatever someone posts, it has to be assumed that it will be seen by everyone. Even if your athlete tries to make a post private or temporary, like on Snapchat, where posts are supposed to be erased, those posts will be circulating long after they are ostensibly deleted. As I explained in chapter 2, there are all sorts of ways to save that snap and pass it along. The next thing your athlete knows, his or her naked body has gone viral. Awkward!

Sure, the situation is not fair, but that's not the point. When someone posts something to social media, that person, perhaps unwittingly but always voluntarily, gives up control of the message or image. He or she will not know where it goes, who sees it, or who reposts it and with what new spin. It is safer for your athlete to just assume that his or her private life is over once he or she starts using social media. Your athlete's business is now everyone's playground.

MYTH 6: I HAVE FREEDOM OF SPEECH, SO I CAN SAY AND DO WHAT I WANT

You and your athlete do have freedom of speech, but neither of you is free from consequences. Every action, whether it is a physical behavior, speech, or the posting of words, comes with positive or negative consequences and sometimes both. Although people can say anything they want in the United States, it does not mean that what they say is not going to be met with some reaction. Make sure the reactions you and your athletes inspire are positive. Negative consequences have far greater impact than positive ones do; negative reactions not only come immediately from the readers of your post, but they also have more lasting repercussions. Remind your athletes that people will forget all of the good that they do, but people will be quick to remember nearly all of your athletes' past transgressions. For example, Cardale Jones may go on to do a lot of great things in the NFL, but he will live the rest of his life as the guy who went to college but only wanted to play football and not go to class.

THE (ALMOST) FINAL WORD ON MYTHS

If you and your athletes become aware of the myths surrounding social media for athletes, you will be a step ahead in the social media game. There are certainly more myths than these, such as "social media has no effect on recruiting." As you will discover, this myth is completely false. Today's recruits are paying attention to social media. They want to know who gets them and who is living in the past. Yes, traditional recruiting tactics still have a place, but now social media is forcing everyone to redraw the x's and o's on the recruiting whiteboard. Let's take a closer look at social media's effect on recruiting now.

4

RECRUITING

We are living in what I term a *micromarketing world*, meaning that people, especially student athletes, no longer want to be pursued as part of a larger group. Rather, they want to be recognized as individuals. They also want to see who is going to play the communication game with them on social media. Which coaches will give them the attention they want and believe they deserve? If you do not do enough to publicly engage with recruits, they will go with the coach and program that will give them that positive public attention. You, as coaches and administrators, need to be prepared for this new reality, because this mindset is not going to go away; instead, it is only going to get more intense. The new digital social media world is changing the way you do business, adding complexity to an already complicated career. You must be prepared for it, because this is the future of recruiting. Do not neglect or ignore social media. If you do, I promise, not being part of the digital world will cost you, if it hasn't already.

The most famous coach-versus-recruit social media battle in the history of NCAA athletics as of this writing happened very recently. The incident started when a top quarterback recruit tweeted that he was decommitting from Texas A&M. Aaron Moorehead, assistant coach for the Texas A&M Aggies, went to Twitter a few minutes later with the following tweet. (All of these tweets have been deleted from Aaron Moorehead's Twitter account, @Amo8685. However, the tweets had already been seen, shared, and saved. As I've said before, nothing truly dies on the Internet!)

> I feel sorry for ppl who never understand loyalty. I can't really even vibe with u. At the end of the day trust is 💯 & everything else is BS
>
> — Aaron Moorehead (@Amo8685) May 5, 2016

Granted, no name was mentioned. However, because of the timing, readers deduced whom Coach Moorehead referred to. Clearly angry and upset about the loss of the recruit, Coach Moorehead continued to allow his emotions to get the best of him as he continued to tweet:

Aaron Moorehead
@Amo8685   ☆   ⚬ Follow

Scared for this next group of kids. There is no accountability and no sense of positivity when it comes to adversity. #selfish #allaboutme

RETWEETS   LIKES
130   233

8:40 PM - 4 May 2016

 **Aaron Moorehead**
@Amo8685   ⚙   Follow

I wasn't even talking about who everyone
thinks I'm talking about. I didn't even know
#badtiming #relevanttho #stillnoloyalty

RETWEETS   LIKES
60   141

9:00 PM - 4 May 2016

↩   ↻   ♥   •••

Although Coach Moorehead attempted to deny that he was
referring to the specific recruit, he continued to use provoc-
ative hashtags like #relevantho and #stillnoloyalty. This
made his denial suspect at best. Still, he continued:

 **Aaron Moorehead**
@Amo8685   ⚙   Follow

People talk about leadership and this
generation flip flops like its nothing. That's a
real issue. My dad would have whipped my ass

RETWEETS   LIKES
115   231

9:10 PM - 4 May 2016

↩   ↻   ♥   •••

Then the fallout happened.

That was followed by even more fallout, as another future recruit indicated he was no longer interested in being pursued by Texas A&M.

The comments continued from Coach Moorehead despite these losses. Once reality set in, though—he may have been called by the head coach, another coach, an administrator, or maybe all three!—he wrote the following apology:

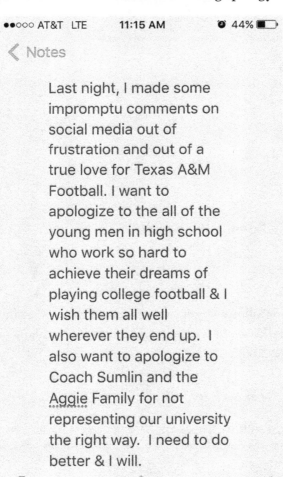

Head Coach Kevin Sumlin was put in the position of having to answer questions concerning his assistant coach. The last thing a head coach wants to deal with when trying to prepare for an upcoming season is unnecessary drama like this.

This entire situation could have been avoided if Coach Moorehead had simply not allowed his emotions to get the best of him and then tweeted his frustration. Such restraint may not have stopped the initial recruit from leaving, but perhaps it could have prevented another recruit from either decommitting or asking to be removed from consideration. The coach's emotions got the best of him. In his defense, loyalty and perseverance are good things. However, in the context of social media, he was making a from-the-gut statement from his perspective as a coach who had been freshly wounded by a young person who had decided to change his direction. This is the problem when it comes to expressing yourself on social media: your viewpoint and feelings are not other people's viewpoints and feelings. Unequivocally declaring yours can be problematic, because doing so can alienate people who might have a reason to sympathize with the other side or who are turned off or frightened by your lack of control, no matter how much of your passion springs from positive sentiments like love and loyalty. The lesson you should learn from Coach Moorehead's mistake is this: Your viewpoint and feelings are yours and yours alone. Keep them to yourself. Know what plays you can and cannot call on the social media field.

As a coach, you have to make some decisions when it comes to social media, because you have to decide what type of players you want to have on your team. I know you are looking for the best talent. However, if the best talent comes with bad social media habits, that talent may not be worth the public relations hit you and your program will take with a troublemaker on board. Part of your job as a coach in the digital era will be to psychologically profile potential recruits through their social media use. As if recruiting was not hard enough already! Now you have to be a social media psychological profiler! Relax! The good news is that everything you need to see is just waiting for you online. Read through your potential recruit's social media and form a judgment about it. There's no interview during which you have to try to see through any half-truths, obfuscation, or Oscar-worthy acting. Simply take a look at what's already on Twitter, Facebook, Instagram, or whatever platforms the recruit uses, and observe how people react to it. What do you think? Can you and your program handle what that recruit dishes out? See further discussion in the Monitoring Future Recruits section of chapter 8.

Social media has also changed recruiting because it has changed personal relationships and, by extension, the dynamics of recruiting. In the old days, the roles of and boundaries between coaches and athletes were quite clear. That is, coaches might scout and instruct athletes, but they did not interact with recruits more than was required to do the business of figuring out whether an athlete was a good fit for a coach's program, and coaches certainly didn't socialize. These days, young women and men want you to be a Facebook friend or one of their Twitter followers. Not only that, but they want you to respond to their posts. This new expectation is a game changer. No longer do they pursue you because they want to be part of your program: they want you to pursue them! They want to see if and how much you really want them to become part of your team. During this strange recruiting ritual, if you say the wrong thing, they move on to another college or university. If you do not acknowledge their value or treat them the way they wish to be treated, they leave.

Enter the new NCAA rules regarding how coaches are allowed to react to recruits' posts. The rule change (Proposal 2015-48) went into effect on August 1, 2016, and reads as follows:

> *An athletics department staff member may take actions (e.g., "like," "favorite," republish, "tag," etc.) on social media platforms that indicate approval of content on social media platforms that was generated by users of the platforms other than institutional staff members or representatives of an institution's athletics interests.*[3]

What does this do? It signals that a new era in recruiting has emerged. Recruits are paying attention to which coaches and programs give them the most attention. Here are a few comments from prospective recruits regarding the rule change:[4]

> *I guess now we can see how much love these schools genuinely have for us (laughing emoji)*

> *Sounds good with me, because I really want to see how much interest they have*

> *Good (flexing arm emoji). At least they will notice me (crying laughing emoji) (100 emoji)*

This is the new world for coaches and administrators. Colleges and universities are scrambling to put together social media teams (often made up of graduate assistants) to look for anything recruits might say on these platforms that they can like, retweet, or tag and thereby give a recruit some extra attention. A social media–savvy small college or university now has an opportunity to land a top-rated recruit simply by paying more attention to that prospective student athlete than a larger university can. This also means that you as coaches cannot blindly attempt to use these social media platforms without understanding them and their potential pitfalls. I've already given you some insight into the various platforms in chapter 2. Keep reading for the heads-up on some social media situations to avoid.

5

CULTURAL INSENSITIVITY, OUTRIGHT NEGATIVITY, AND OTHER GAFFES

As we saw with Coach Moorehead, making sweeping, emotional proclamations can be problematic. So can stepping on someone's culture. Even a post with innocent intentions can put administrators in an awkward position.

Take, for example, a Cinco de Mayo tweet from the football office at Iowa State University. Someone Photoshopped the faces of three of the program's star football players over those of Steve Martin, Chevy Chase, and Martin Short on the movie poster of the 1980s comedy *The Three Amigos*, then tweeted it with the program's wishes for everyone to have a happy Cinco de Mayo. Some people responded by pointing out that the photo was culturally insensitive, and the tweet was pulled down. As you know by now, though, the deletion was too late; the poster is available online and will be forever. Jamie Pollard, the athletic director, had to issue a public statement apologizing for the tweet.

As the *Ames Tribune* reported, head coach Campbell and his staff had tried to be "cutting edge with their use of images and social media since he was hired"—using images from

Star Wars and *Game of Thrones*, for example—but this was a case of misjudgment.[5] I am sure no one meant for the tweet to be culturally insensitive, nor did anyone intend to hurt or harm anyone else. However, in today's social media world, everyone is paying attention to everything, especially when it comes to athletics. Even when you think you are doing everything right, even though your intentions are innocent, things can still go wrong on social media. This doesn't mean that you shouldn't use social media. It only means that you can mean well but still put your athletic department into a situation that it shouldn't be in if you aren't careful. However, by being aware of possible problems and by following the strategies outlined in this book, you will precipitously reduce the likelihood of accidentally creating such situations.

Beware of the Haters

Social media is truly a new world of different rules, different expectations, different languages, different norms, and multiple cultures. Communicating with people online is surprisingly different from how people communicate face-to-face. Tone of voice, facial expressions, and gestures are not available to communicate nonverbal positivity or nuance. Also, as with any social group, followers of athletic social media include some bad actors just waiting to capitalize on any little thing they can to exploit a college, a coach, an athlete, or a program. They are lurking, ready to pounce on any post, picture, or video, no matter how seemingly insignificant. You, as a coach or administrator, need to learn about your opponents in cyberspace, just as you would prepare for the team your squad is about to meet in its next matchup. Whether or

not you choose to use these social media platforms personally, most of your athletes will be using them, so you need to
understand not so much how each platform works (although
it helps) but how people react on social media so you can
anticipate problems before they occur and even harness the
technology for your own or your program's purposes.

I recall playing football in college. I remember the practices.
I remember how I hated hot Nebraska August days. I also
remember how we were pushed, the words that were said.
Some of the words slung at us by coaches were not so flat-
tering, to put it mildly. At that time, taking the verbal abuse
was just part of the deal. We may have been angry about
being talked to in that way, but we took it because it was
culturally accepted then, and we really wanted to both play
the game and improve as players. Today, how coaches interact with players is different. Is it because the players are
more sensitive? Is it because it is less culturally acceptable
to scream at players? Is it because the digital world has in-
fluenced our emotions so much that by saying something in
a strong way causes players to move from one program to
another? Perhaps it is a combination of all of these things.
The point is that you need to be aware of all of these factors
and adjust your communication style accordingly, especially if you want to be successful on social media.

6

THE SMARTPHONE AND THE NOT-SO-SMART PEOPLE USING IT

Everyone has a phone, and almost everyone has some form of a smartphone. The phones may be smart, but I sometimes wonder about the people who use them. After all, the phones themselves don't create problems; the people pressing the buttons do. Fewer people are carrying around and using a laptop, some of you or your student athletes may use a tablet, but the phone is the primary social media tool. It is the device most commonly used to check social media feeds, take pictures, record videos, and post. A number of social media platforms, like Snapchat and Instagram, are smartphone-only applications. In short, the smartphone is a powerful communication tool. However, for some, it offers the opportunity to make themselves famous.

People want their moment of fame. Fame enhances their own self-esteem, and they believe it earns the esteem of others. Those who either do not have the talent to become famous in their own right or have not discovered where their talent lies will often have their phones at the ready to give them an opportunity to record a candid image or event that could go viral or otherwise gain them notoriety but begin a major headache for you. Consider the videos that you watch on YouTube, Facebook, Snapchat, Instagram, or even Twitter. For the most part, they are not recorded on a camera; they are being taken by and posted from a smartphone. People are just waiting to capture someone saying or doing something wrong, stupid, funny, or crazy. They are waiting for someone to fail. Athletes can especially be targets, not so much for what they do on the field but what they do off the field. You and your student athletes have to be careful everywhere you go so that you don't become fodder for these amateur videographers.

Not so long ago, athletes didn't have to worry about phones with cameras. They had to worry about a graduate assistant coach showing up at the party they should not be attending. Now, every person has the potential to send you, the coach, a video of your athletes' bad behavior or, perhaps worse yet, post it on some social media platform. Your athletes may think they are going out in public to have a good time, but, while there, they do not think about or realize they are being photographed or filmed. Sometimes they may let themselves be filmed or photographed and not think it is a big deal. Usually it is not. Chances are, though, that eventually someone will take a picture or record a video that your athlete or you will not want posted. Maybe your athlete got loud and obnoxious when he was drunk, or maybe she raised her arm to wave at a friend but had a picture snapped at a very inopportune time, such that the wave looks like a Nazi salute. Even more likely is that you and your athlete won't know that this picture or video exists until after it has been posted and the fallout is raining down on both of you.

The other problematic scenario occurs when your athlete is attending a party where something goes wrong. Your athlete hasn't done anything wrong, so he or she decides to leave the situation, because your athlete does not want to be a part of the drama. Too late! Someone has taken a video or a picture of your athlete at the party. He or she cannot escape the evidence of his or her presence. Your athlete denies doing anything wrong, but because your athlete was at the party when things went wrong, your athlete is now guilty by association. Depending on the nature of the incident, someone else's phone can have you and your athlete called downtown to the local police department to answer questions, even when your athlete didn't do anything! I know, it's not fair, but that is the power of someone else's phone. Athletes need to not to put themselves in those situations. However, you and I both know that is not the way that young people think. I was in college, and I know I found myself in more than one situation that I should have not been in, but my friends were there so I was too. I suspect you can recall similar experiences from your own college days. Lucky for us, no one had a smartphone then.

Yet smartphones are not all bad, especially if you can get your athletes to use their phones for good causes. Encourage them to take pictures with your team's fans and document their visits to the local children's hospital. Let them know that it's OK to allow people to snap a picture with them when they are walking through campus. Most of the time, pictures and videos are sources of fun and positive PR rather than problems for your team. However, when your athletes are off campus, even if they are eating at a restaurant with a date, they need to be aware that everyone has a phone, everyone is watching, and some people are willing to steal someone's pride so they can become famous, even if it is for just a couple of seconds.

7

MAKING THE RIGHT SOCIAL MEDIA RULES FOR YOUR TEAM

I hope that after reading this, you haven't decided to change career paths! You are likely already thinking about how you might control this thing called social media. You are possibly even considering making some rules for your staff and your athletes. I do not have a problem with rules per se, especially because that responsibility does ultimately fall to you as the head coach. The tougher part of this equation is that you also have to get your team to buy into your vision of what constitutes appropriate social media use. But take heart: different coaches have enacted different social media policies—some strict, some not so much—and both approaches have been successful.

For example, the University of Connecticut women's basketball team has a policy of no Twitter from the first day practice starts until after the season is over. I don't have to tell you how successful the UConn women's basketball team is. The young women do not fight the policy, but, then again, it is hard to argue with the team's success. Who would want to rock that team's boat? Does that mean that a no-Twitter policy is responsible for their success? No. However, the absence of Twitter means the players have one less distraction during their season. Everyone is on the same page, no one is treated differently, and the players probably spend more time than most team members do actually talking to each other, seeing as how they are not buried in their phones.

Coach Kirk Ferentz, the head football coach at the University of Iowa, has a zero-Twitter policy as well. For him, it makes life easier as a coach. Is this policy well liked by the team? Probably not, but then again, he is the head coach. The players need to follow his rules. Players understand that even though they might not like curfews and other off-the-field rules, they need to respect them. Social media restrictions are just another set of rules that players abide by. Other football programs, such as Clemson, have instituted similar social media bans while in season. It is an option to consider. However, I caution you to think carefully about instituting such a policy before lowering the boom, because it is often difficult for players to follow what they see as a draconian rule.

A different way of handling the issue is practiced by the football team at the University of Alabama. Nick Saban has a fairly simple rule: If you (as a student athlete) act responsibly, you can use social media. (http://www.al.com/sports/index.ssf/2012/08/nick_saban_explains_his_alabam.html) If you abuse it, then the football staff will take more control. The football staff monitor all of the social media activity of their players. In general, problems have been minimal, and the team has met with great success on the field of play. Monitoring may not be practical for many institutions, because the number of players and the hours of monitoring require extra personnel. However, if you are in a situation where you can monitor your athletes' social media, this is an example of how individuals can still be allowed to use social media without interrupting the team's success. See chapter 8 for more about social media monitoring.

Regardless of what direction you choose to go in regarding your student athletes' social media use, make the decision and stick with it. If you choose to shut it off at the beginning of the season, then do not let up midyear. If you allow your players to use social media in season, then trying to take it away in the middle of the season will be more of distraction than if you let them continue. In short, changing the rules in the middle of the season or not having clear social media policies will rock your moving boat—don't change directions midstream.

ASSISTANT COACHES AND GRADUATE ASSISTANT COACHES:
YOU ARE IMPORTANT!

I have been around and worked for many different college and university athletic departments. My experiences at these institutions lead me to make the bold prediction that if you are an assistant coach or a graduate assistant coach reading this book, chances are pretty good that you are doing so for your head coach and that you will be summarizing everything I am saying for your head coach once you finish it. I promise I will provide a summary at the end to help make your reporting easier. Keep reading, though, because you will need to fill in the details.

I also suspect, graduate assistant coaches, that you are younger than your head coach and possibly the other coaches, too. Depending on the age of your head coach, you likely have a tremendous advantage when it comes to social media because you have been around it more, probably use it, and have a pretty good handle on how the platforms work. However, that being said, knowing how a platform works is not enough. Also, you probably understand better than any of your older coaches just how much of a positive tool social media can be for your sports program. I am relying on you to help me convince your head coach that social media can be beneficial, even though some dangers do exist.

As a younger member of your coaching staff, you need to be instrumental in guiding the young people you work with on their use of social media. Older coaches often do not understand social media and therefore ignore it or simply do not concern themselves with it. I don't blame them. They have bigger things on their minds. Because you are closer to the athletes in age and have more experience with social media, you are the logical choice to be the go-to guide and advisor for the team's social media use. Here is an opportunity for you to transition from former player to honest-to-goodness coach!

Perhaps it has not been long since you were the athlete, but now you have this coaching responsibility. Maybe you have had your own issues using social media. You may feel that you have no right to tell these young people what to do and what not to do because you have not been the best example. Relax. Use your own experiences as teaching moments, the same way you would use your failures in your sport. Tell your athletes what you learned. Be honest with them. I promise you, they will respect you more, they will trust you greatly, and you will get more out of them than you ever expected if you are up-front and even a bit vulnerable with them about your failure. Sharing failures may seem counterintuitive, but we all learn from failure. If we can pass the lessons we learned the hard way along to our students and athletes, even if only one accepts our instruction, we have made an amazing change in someone's life. Sometimes you can do good by serving as a bad example. Perhaps you will help someone avoid a disaster. For many of these young athletes, their phones and social media are extensions of themselves, yet they are still figuring out the right ways to use them. Take advantage of your position to guide them, teach them, and continually train them.

This may seem like a role reversal, but you must also be ready to train your fellow coaches. Even if they do not want to be a part of social media, coaches must be aware of what it is, who is on it, and how to use it responsibly so they can develop a social media policy or at least lay some ground rules for the players and coaching staff. Just because they ignore social media does not mean they do not or should not have an influence on how it is used by members of the team and the coaching staff. Give them the quick overview of the platforms that I have provided for you in chapter 2. Update your coaches with a "what's trending" view of your team by telling them what the team members are saying on social media. Your team members' posts can give you great insight into where the heads of individual players are at any given time as well as the overall emotional and mental state of the team. By sharing the views of the team and then teaching the coaches how to make these observations themselves, you can help your coaches in a truly significant way.

Help your head coach understand how important social media is to recruit and reach young people. Coaches often underestimate just how much impact one retweet, one like, or one tag can have on a young person. On August 1, 2016, an NCAA rule change went into effect to allow coaches to like, retweet, share, and tag recruits' posts, and coaches have been doing so enthusiastically. If nothing else, consider whether getting more likes, retweets, and other social media feedback is going to make a young recruit feel bad. No! On the contrary, the attention only encourages that recruit to post more, and laying a foundation of support for a prospective recruit may help convince the recruit to attend your program when decision time rolls around. I believe the social media give-and-take will become a game, and I am convinced that we are very close to witnessing the first athlete to choose a school on the basis of the number of likes, retweets, and tags he or she has received from that college's coach. Sound crazy? Yet, at the same time, did we ever think that talking online would influence so many decisions in the real world? Trust me when I say it is coming.

In short, be your head coach's eyes on social media. You also need to reverse roles and be your coach's coach when it comes to social media. If you can do these things well, you will have increased your value on the market when you become a head coach. You will also have an advantage that older coaches and coaches who do not want to be involved with social media do not have. The more you understand the psychology of how and why people do what they do on these platforms, the better your professional position, because your special insight raises your stock and increases your value to the institution that hires you.

8

SOCIAL MEDIA MONITORING: IS IT WORTH IT?

One of the most difficult tasks for coaches today is monitoring their athletes' social media. If you are new to social media monitoring, let me just say that it can be done, and sometimes even relatively inexpensively. Chances are that you will have an assistant or perhaps a team of people to help you monitor your current student athletes' social media as well as future recruits' social media. There are online applications such as Varsity Monitor that institutions can pay for, but you can also use a platform like the professional version of Hootsuite to monitor social media activity as well. However, several monitoring issues are far more difficult to handle than finding the right software.

THE CHALLENGES OF MONITORING YOUR ATHLETES

The first and most important issue you will have when it comes to monitoring your athletes' social media is knowing who on your team uses social media, which social media platforms they are using, and what their screen names are. This all seems quite manageable if you have a basketball program consisting of fourteen players. But if fourteen players are using four different platforms each, that means you are trying to keep track of fifty-six different accounts. Can you imagine the task you're facing if you have 100 football players? You potentially need to have someone or a team of people monitoring 400 accounts, and that assumes your players don't have multiple accounts on each platform.

Another issue is actually identifying all of your athletes' accounts. You may have access to what you think is all of their social media, but some players may have created profiles that are not associated with their names but that their friends know so they can continue posting without your oversight. Your players may tell you about only the platforms they want you to see. Finally, other social media platforms are out there that are not even mentioned here because they are so new that they are somewhat of a mystery. One such example is a platform called Kik. Little is known about its impact. It is not clear how many people actively use it. Even as much as I research these platforms, it is nearly impossible to keep up with all of them, not to mention their secret applications. They grow quickly. Some end quickly as well. In the end, it's hard to monitor what you don't even know exists.

Now it gets even more tricky, because you have to be allowed by your athlete to see the social media accounts you're supposed to monitor, assuming they did not preemptively block you through their privacy settings. You cannot force them to give you access. Even if you do get through all of their permissions and privacy settings, as I've already mentioned, who is going to watch everything that is posted? You're busy coaching, so you don't have time for this full-time-plus job.

This is why so many coaches have the rule "You can use it as long as you don't abuse it." It is also why other coaches have a zero-social-media rule. Monitoring is manageable, but it is not by any means an easy task. What is more, monitoring is all post hoc, meaning that even though you are watching, you may not actually be preventing anything. By definition, monitoring social media is reactionary in nature, and its reach is limited to what is being monitored.

For example, suppose you have all of the monitoring tools set up for your team. You are tracking everything your athletes say and do on all of the social media platforms they use. Well, suppose one athlete's "friend" decides to post on some Sunday at 3:00 a.m. on his or her own (not the athlete's) Facebook page a picture of the athlete smoking a bowl of marijuana at a party. When that picture turns up on the local news station or sports station the next day, you might be angry at the monitor, but what could the monitor have done? In reality, nothing would have prevented that photo from making the news. The photo wasn't posted to a monitored page, so you could not expect the monitor to see it. Assuming the monitor had seen the picture as soon as it was posted, what was he or she to do? Nothing. It wasn't posted on the athlete's monitored account, so the monitor would have had no authority to have the poster take the picture down. Even if the athlete posted the picture on her or his Facebook page, the monitor still had little effective recourse. He or she could have tried to call the offending athlete, but such an action would have been too late anyway, as someone would surely have already captured the photo on a screenshot from their phone, tablet, or computer.

This is why monitoring provides a false sense of security. By monitoring athletes' social media, we are not preventing young women and men from posting stupid things; we are merely reacting to those dumb posts. And guess who is going to have to answer to the media for something an athlete did on social media while on your team? YOU! Oh, monitoring may lessen the frequency of poorly considered posts a little, but monitoring is just not all that effective at prevention. Rather, it is important and potentially more effective to continually educate and remind athletes how to use social media correctly and responsibly to avoid letting the horse out of the barn in the first place. This is also why your social media rules, how you are going to enforce them, and what consequences are going to be associated with inappropriate social media use need to be strategized and put in writing up front. Reacting is not the way to handle social media. Be proactive. Know what you need to know and stand by your rules.

MONITORING FUTURE RECRUITS

Perhaps where monitoring has an advantage is in recruiting your next athletes. Reading what a young person says on social media can tell you all you need to know about what type of person you will get if you recruit him or her. This is all about your tolerance level for shenanigans and the potential fallout you are willing to deal with as a coach. If you are not monitoring your recruits' behavior on social media, I suggest you start immediately. By doing so, you can save yourself many potential future social media issues, not to mention real-world issues stemming from errors in judgment and immaturity. If your recruit demonstrates his or her character on social media, you will have that much more information to factor into your recruiting decisions. Of course, you still may not see everything this athlete posts or every aspect of his or her personality, but at least by doing your due diligence you can be proactive in your recruiting and avoid inviting a student athlete who would not be a good fit to your program.

Evaluating an athlete on the basis of his or her social media behavior may seem unfair. However, experiencing negative fallout as a result of the poor judgment demonstrated by even one student athlete with a dumb post on social media can raise questions about you as the coach, the program in general, and even the institution. In addition, depending on the severity of what the athlete says or does on social media, your program could become the target of a future investigation either internally or externally via the NCAA. When a student athlete either does not use social media or uses it responsibly, you do not need to worry about such issues.

There is another side to this issue of choosing not to recruit athletes because of what you discover via their social media use. By not recruiting them, you may be doing them one of the biggest favors of their lives. That is, they will experience direct consequences of their social media behavior and perhaps be inspired to take steps to bring it (and their off-the-field behavior that generates material for ill-advised posts) under control. I have read countless social media mentions from coaches who stopped recruiting an athlete on the basis of that athlete's social media behavior. Here are just a few examples:

Penn State

Herb Hand
@CoachHand

Dropped another prospect this AM due to his social media presence...Actually glad I got to see the 'real' person before we offered him.

Duke

Derek Jones @dukecoachdj · 14h
Our jobs depend on the young men that we recruit. Your social media pages say a lot about your character, discipline & common sense. #Ap2w

SMU

Coach Justin Stepp @coachjstepp · Jan 8
Came across an awful Twitter account today. Shame the kid was a really good player...On to the next one...get a clue!

When that happens, you send a young person an extremely strong message that it is not good enough to be a great athlete. In reality, you have to also be a good person. Social media can reveal many things about your prospective recruit that you may have to deal with after you sign him or her. If you aren't liking what you're seeing off the field, you can be a part of a greater life lesson that will help shape that athlete's future.

9

PLAYING OFFENSE ON SOCIAL MEDIA

There are three ways to play when using social media. You can play offense, defense, or—what I recommend—a combination of both. It is important that you as a coach and an administrator as well as your student athletes know a few plays that can make navigating social media successfully easier.

Playing offense on social media is about knowing what works and leaves a positive impression on those reading or otherwise seeing a post. It is a proactive approach that puts you in the driver's seat of social media. Although it is difficult to know if you are advancing down the field or court or whether you have scored, the effort is worth it.

Here I suggest possible types of posts that can create goodwill and social capital among your athletes' followers. I also recommend that you, as coaches and administrators, use these strategies as well. Some of these posts may seem either silly or self-serving, but understand that both leave positive rather than negative impressions on social media users. So often when coaches and administrators talk about social media, they will tell their student athletes what not to do. Yet we all know that is really not coaching; you need to have a plan for what you should do. That said, here are some of my favorite social media plays. Take advantage of them, and encourage your student athletes to do the same.

THE VOLUNTEER PLAY

You may do this already, but chances are you and your athletes will be asked to volunteer for some charity. If the charity aligns with your values, say yes! Use the opportunity to help others to also promote the charitable organization and its cause by taking pictures, recording videos, and talking about the charity. Express what you admire about it, what you enjoyed about helping, why you support the charity, and related sentiments and observations. As people in sports who have a social media presence, you and your athletes are in a position to raise awareness about an issue in a way that can help a charity. Regularly bring up the charity on social media, and show your interaction with the people who run the charity and the people whom the charity helps. There are many great causes in your local area and community. Some examples of ways you and your athletes can help are:

- ▶ Visiting a children's hospital
- ▶ Taking part in a holiday celebration at a senior living center
- ▶ Volunteering at a homeless shelter
- ▶ Building homes for Habitat for Humanity
- ▶ Reading books for children at a local school
- ▶ Cleaning up after a major storm

These possibilities are just the tip of the iceberg. Beyond the actual labor provided for the cause, good works put athletes in a tremendously positive light. They move beyond being just athletes and instead are elevated to the position of being a positive example for others to emulate. You may already be doing this. Great! Do not stop helping out, and make sure you are sharing your good works on social media.

THE TRAVEL PLAY

Your athletes get to do something that a typical college student does not generally do in the course of the school year: travel. You may not think traveling is a big deal, but to many people, it is a huge deal. Why is this? A psychologist might tell you that there are two reasons. First, people are curious. Second, people like vicariously through the lives of others. Have you ever noticed how many TV shows there are about eating and traveling and traveling in general? Entire TV stations are devoted to showing viewers other parts of the country or world. Why? Because, as humans, we are interested in the novel, we dream, we consider whether this exotic-to-us locale is a place we want to go. People—not just family and friends, but strangers and fans—want to accompany you and the team on your travels and see the world through your eyes. You will find that not only will posts from the road get more likes and comments than those from home, but people are more likely to share your posts about your travels, too. If you do allow social media in season, here are some examples of fun travel posts:

- ► Wefies (group selfies) on the plane or bus
- ► Pictures of the first thing the team sees when they escape the airport

► Pictures of historical or interesting sites
► Pictures of the field or court they are about to compete on
► Pictures of team meals

Again, the possibilities are endless.

THE SELFIE WEFIE STRATEGY

What? Selfies? Yes, selfies and wefies. I recently alluded to *wefies*, or group selfies. Yes, people do like selfies and wefies. Your athletes take them, so why not encourage them to post positive selfies and wefies? For that matter, why don't you take some of your own? Here are some suggested pictures for posting:

► Pictures of your student athletes (alone or in small groups) in their uniforms
► Pictures of the entire team in their uniforms or street clothes
► Pictures of you or your student athletes with fans
► Pictures of the student athletes with you or their other coaches
► Pictures or video of unique or fun training methods used with your athletes

Yes, they may seem a bit narcissistic, but selfies and wefies help make social media fun. Oh, and by the way, they do not always have to be serious! They can be silly, intense, or somewhere in between. Humans like seeing other humans having fun. So make sure that you and your team show us the fun side of your organization and your sport!

THE DOCUMENTARY PLAY

Previously, I talked to you about the travel play. You can take that play a step further to what I call the *documentary play*. Humans are interested in what others do, not just where they go. This may sound crazy, but many people think that being a college athlete or coach is easy. They believe, wrongly, that you live this plush life, the athletes do not go to class, the sport is all play, and life is smooth sailing. Want to correct that impression? Tell us the behind-the-scenes story. As humans, we love stories. Show people what life in the athletic program is really like. Create a video (or challenge your team to shoot one) about what it is like to go through a day as a coach or a student athlete: waking up exhausted, staying up late, and watching film until the wee hours of the morning, not to mention the little time you get to spend with your family, the meetings, the preparation, the booster meetings, the special engagements you have to do, the recruiting trail, and so on. (For a great example, see the Hayes for Days series by Nigel Hayes on the Wisconsin Badgers channel on YouTube.) Perhaps you can even take fans through the day before a game and show how you and the team prepare (without giving away too many trade secrets, of course). You may think no one cares about this stuff. However, people do care, more than you realize. The fans will love your inside scoop and you will educate them at the same time. Plus, by making this documentary play, you could even be unknowingly auditioning for TV work during your postcoaching career.

PRACTICE DRILLS

One of the NFL Network's most popular broadcasts is their NFL combine drills. With the advent of YouTube and all of the other social media video options, you as a coach have an opportunity to demonstrate your preseason preparations by filming and posting practice drills, maybe even with your commentary. This is a great offensive play for three reasons. First, it shows recruits what they need to prepare for. Second, it also shows your recruits how you are evaluating them. Finally, as the NFL Network combine ratings prove, fans are interested in drills as well as in official in-season play. These videos do not have to be long, and you can streamline them for the platform you're posting to. You can post a ten-second shot on Snapchat or a minute-long video on, say, Instagram. (And the sky's the limit for YouTube!) Give the general public and your future recruits a taste of what is to come and show them how you pursue excellence.

DANCING COACHES

This next suggestion may be pushing you out of your comfort zone, but hear me out. Do you like it when your team wins? Of course you do. What do you do when the clock sits on zeros, or the final out is made, or your team has the most points on the scoreboard? You think you might be happy enough to dance? I'm here to tell you to not only go for it but have someone record it so you can post it! One of the most-seen viral college sports–related videos of recent memory featured Dabo Swinney, the head coach of the Clemson Tigers, dancing with other coaches and players after a victory. On YouTube alone it has over 120,000 views; add in the Vine videos and moveable GIFs on the other social media platforms and you've got exponentially more views. Do you think a recruit saw this and thought that Clemson would be a fun place to play football? Maybe this video is not the only reason a recruit would think that

Clemson would be a good place to play, but I promise you it certainly added to the attraction.

Not everyone is comfortable dancing. Yet for a dancing coach video, a lack of dancing skill might be a better viewer draw. If you are willing, this silly-sounding type of post has a tendency to go viral in a good way. These particular videos are powerful because they represent such a departure from what people think of when they contemplate coaches. These videos also demonstrate that a coach has a human, fun side. It is hard not to smile and even laugh when you see a coach trying dance after a win. Of course, whether you take up this challenge is up to you. Here is a fact, we love seeing coaches in their moments of joy. So, while you may not be the next candidate for "Dancing with the Stars," you might find that your moves can cause a recruit to see you as more authentic.

OTHER SUGGESTED POSTS

You may have had difficulty figuring out what to post that makes sense for you, your team, your program, and your school. The truth is, when it comes to social media, the key is just being you. Be intentional, but be the good human being that you are. Talk about the great things your athletes do. Talk about what an awesome staff or administration you work for. Talk about the new facilities or the upgrades happening around you. Talk about your life as a coach when you can. Tell us about how excited you are for the season to start. The positive topics available for you to talk about are endless. It is all in how you look at the world. It doesn't mean that negative things do not exist, but focus on the positive things and share them. Such a focus on positivity will not only brighten your outlook, but it will also have people thinking good things about your program.

Just One Example of a Great Offense

Marcus Paige played basketball for the University of North Carolina. He and the North Carolina Tar Heels fell short in the 2016 national championship game against Villanova, losing on a last-second shot at the end of regulation time. However, if you want to see an example of someone who has played great social media offense, go to Marcus's Twitter profile: @marcuspaige5. He talks about all sorts of subjects, takes pictures and videos, and is having a great time on Twitter. He has over 324,000 followers at the time of this writing, and I expect that number will only go up, whether he ultimately ends up in the NBA, on television as a sports commentator, or elsewhere for what is sure to be a stellar professional career. His use of social media is making him a star, right now for the Alt Lake City Stars NBA D-League , but it could just as well be company who would love to have them as part of their brand. If you take a moment to look through his Twitter posts, you will find a great example of someone who plays at an incredibly high level both on the court and in social media.

Is this a result of Marcus Paige understanding how to use social media or was he trained in its use? My belief is that his success can be credited to a combination of both who he is as a person and what he has learned from the mistakes of others. There is no substitute for character. Although I do not know Marcus personally, just reading his history of tweets on Twitter indicates to me that he understands the nature of what to do and what not to do on social media.

There are more student athletes who use social media responsibly than those who do not. The problem is that the few who do use it inappropriately stand out. Their bad behavior on social media makes the news. It is sad that so many people can do the right thing when it comes to social media, but they are eclipsed by the few who make such a mess of it. This is why the knee-jerk reaction of coaches and administrators when a student athlete messes up on social media is often a quick, wide-reaching, and severe rescinding of social media privileges for entire teams or even across teams. I understand why banning social media appears to be a reasonable response, but at the same time, I do not want you to dump social media for your entire team or athletic program because one or two students exhibit poor judgment. You as a coach, your program, and your athletic department will benefit if you have articulate and enthusiastic athletes tweeting and posting about the excellent athletics to be found at your school.

Encourage your team to use the offensive social media plays found in this chapter. If you suggest and support these strategies, then your student athletes are less apt to do the wrong thing on social media. It is hard to do wrong when you are in the middle of doing right. The two behaviors are incompatible. Do not be afraid to give your players some ideas for positive posts so that they can begin to formulate their own creative approaches to each social media offense strategy. For those times when a defensive strategy may be more appropriate, though, turn to the next chapter.

10

PLAYING DEFENSE ON SOCIAL MEDIA

When you play offense on social media, you are trying to score positive social capital with the world around you. There will also be times, though, when you will need to play social media defense. We have all heard it said—and we know it is true—that defense wins championships. However, sometimes we have to play defense out of necessity. Here are some defensive social media plays that you may want to consider when events make playing defense necessary.

GAME LOSS ZONE DEFENSE

One of the things I really love about Marcus Paige's Twitter feed is that he did not post after North Carolina lost a championship game to Villanova. That was a smart defensive move. After a loss, especially a critical one, players and coaches are emotional. After all, athletes and coaches are competitive, and with that competitiveness comes the pain of losing, which hurts more than winning feels good. You hate it. Every athlete and coach does. Knowing that, it becomes obvious that when you and your athletes are in that angry, hurt, want-to-scream-at-the-world-how-you-feel zone, you need to play defense and not post anything on social media.

It is a great play for a variety of reasons. First, some people love to kick other people when they are down or angry. As a matter of fact, the psychological term *schadenfreude* refers to pleasure from other people's misery or pain. Trust me, those people who experience schadenfreude are out there. You may think of them as trolls, haters, or worse, but they are looking for an athlete or a coach to lose and post about it so they can rub the loss in. Yes, it is cruel. I wish I could tell you such behavior is the modus operandi of just a few unkind people, but the fact is, based on trending numbers, there are potentially tens of thousands if not more social media users out there who are just waiting to laugh at and take advantage of the pain of others. To avoid making yourself or your team the target of such unpleasant people, when you or your athletes are in that painful zone, play the defense of not posting.

THE CORNER BLITZ

The corner blitz occurs when out of nowhere, someone who thinks that he or she is clever rips into you, your family, your team, your teammate, another coach, an athlete, or your school. You never saw it coming. All of sudden, BAM! This post comes out of nowhere and nearly knocks the wind out of you. Because it is so personal, it leaves you stunned and angry. In response to such uncalled-for aggression, you must do what you tell your athletes to do on the field when they get hit hard by an opponent or are on the bad end of a lousy call by a referee: Bite your lip. Walk away. Move on to the next play. Above all, do not let the poster know you are hurt. By not responding, you rob the poster of the satisfaction of knowing that he or she got to you. The best revenge is to move on without acknowledging the hit. Leave it alone. Remember, if you don't feed the trolls, they will die.

TEAM DEFENSE

There will be times, either during your season or for the entire school year, that you as a coaching staff decide that you and your team are going to turn off all social media. An alternative strategy would be to turn off a specific social media platform, such as Twitter. I call this *team defense*, because you are more than likely making this decision as a group of coaches for the good of the entire team and coaching staff, so that all of you can avoid any possible distractions resulting from one team member's or coach's social media posts. This defense is typically mandated by the coaching staff, but occasionally it is decided by a majority group vote by the team.

A great example of this is the University of Connecticut's women's basketball team. UConn women's basketball is one of the most dominant forces in Division 1 college sports. They have won ten national championships since 2000 and four consecutive championships since 2013, including the 2016 national championship. Part of their success might be attributable to the fact that Twitter is shut down for the team from the first day of practice to the final day of the season. Typically, the day before practice starts, the UConn women announce on their Twitter accounts something to the effect of "See ya later, Twitter." This strategy may seem extreme to you, but if you ask these champion athletes, they will tell you that the Twitter blackout means that they have one less thing to think about. It allows them to focus on what they need to do with fewer distractions.

Taking a break from social media can be a good thing. Your athletes may feel like they need to be on social media all of the time, but they really do not. As a matter of fact, you will find that the longer they are not on social media, the less stress they feel and the more they are engaged with you, their teammates, and their other coaches. I can understand why young people want to argue against social media blackouts; however, it's hard for them to argue with four national championships in a row. You and your athletes should also know that teams in other sports do the same thing. For example, in 2015, Clemson University football players and coaches closed down their social media during the season, as had become the team's habit. Not everyone on the team liked or agreed with that policy, but they followed it because that is what you do when you are part of a team. Just because a mandate is unpopular doesn't mean that it is the wrong thing to do. It may turn out to be the best thing for the team. Incidentally, after going undefeated in their regular season, Clemson won the 2015 ACC Conference Championship Game, and headed to the National Championship Game where they lost. The following year they returned to the National Championship game in 2016 and won. Coincidence? I will let you be the judge.

DEACTIVATION DEFENSE

The next strategy comes straight from the "Best Offense Is a Good Defense" file. Do you know that there's a sketchy picture, post, or video of one of your players or coaches lurking on the Internet? Do you have the sneaking suspicion that a troll is waiting for the worst possible time to post this bombshell, so that you, your player or coach, and your team are embarrassed and distracted at a time you cannot afford to be? It may be time, then, to try the *deactivation defense*. Let me tell you a story that will illustrate my point.

Laremy Tunsil played left tackle for the University of Mississippi. He was projected to be the first offensive linemen to be selected in the 2016 NFL draft. At one point, he was expected to be the first pick overall. Thirty minutes before the draft started, a video was shared on his Twitter timeline of Tunsil with a gas mask on, smoking a bowl of marijuana. He admitted the video was of him, but he added that it was recorded when he was younger. His value immediately dropped among the NFL teams interested in him. The predicted top draft pick was not even among the top ten; furthermore, he ended up being the third lineman chosen. It has been estimated that this downward movement in the draft cost him millions of dollars.

On the bright side, Tunsil was still picked in the first round. However, the video cost him future money and endorsements. He is also going to have to spend a significant amount of time trying to prove that he does not have off-the-field issues. He is now on what some people say is a short leash: if he does anything else questionable, people are not going to give him the benefit of the doubt. Even though the video was out for less than a couple of minutes, it was quickly saved and reposted all over the Internet by every major news outlet and plenty of individuals. His best defense, one he deployed at the time, was to deactivate his Twitter account. He temporarily deactivated his other accounts as well.

If you have to have an athlete deactivate his or her social media accounts, how long should you have the athlete keep them down? There is no clear answer to this question. Some athletes can deactivate for a year or two, and some have never reactivated their social media accounts. I have noticed that now that he is playing for the Miami Dolphins, Tunsil has reactivated most of his accounts. He is also being very careful about what he posts. Deactivation sounds severe, but it is a great defensive move that lets you stay under the radar, out of the news, and out of trouble. It really is the safest defensive play in the playbook. If you think that there is anything in your athletes' past that could come back to haunt you or them in the future, then running the deactivation defense may be the best play for you and your athletes.

11

HELPING YOUR ATHLETE TAKE THE TIME-OUT AND GO FOR THE WIN

Proactive coaches and administrators need to understand how to prevent student athletes from posting inappropriate things on social media. In my book *The Social Media Playbook for Student Athletes*, I talk about taking a time-out for the WIN. In fact, taking a time-out is the best way for social media users to ensure that they are using social media well. All this entails is pausing for thirty seconds before hitting the "submit" or "post" button after something has been written, photographed, or recorded to make sure that what is going to be released to the world is not offensive and is worthwhile to share.

Thirty seconds sounds like a short time. However, if every athlete and coach would have taken thirty seconds to question whether they should post something they ended up regretting, most of the problems we have seen on social media would never have occurred. Why? Because in thirty seconds, you can take a breath and sort through some of the strong feelings and thoughts driving you to express yourself. If you force yourself to slow your roll and think things through, you have a better shot at preventing yourself from sharing ill-advised, raw, or emotional posts that result in unpleasant and unintended consequences. Time has been called "the great healer," but it is also the great preventer.

In your sport, you call a time-out for a number of reasons. Sometimes thirty seconds is all you need to get your team to regroup, refocus, relax, and reset. The same is true with social media. A simple thirty-second time-out can help social media users regroup their thoughts, refocus on what is important, relax from the intensity of the emotional inspiration for their post, and reset by either erasing the post or coming up with a more positive way of expressing themselves. Do yourself and your team a favor: teach everyone to take a time-out before they actually post.

GO FOR THE WIN

Who doesn't like winning? We all do. Yet it is also true for all humans that losing hurts more than winning feels good. However, some athletes have a hard time focusing on what they could lose if they use social media unwisely. I do not want to be one of those negative people who rattles off a bunch of "thou shalt not's" when it comes to social media. Besides, I, of all people, appreciate the positive side of social media and what it can do for you and your program. When you get down to it, you wouldn't send your athletes onto the field of play without training. Your athletes are going to use social media, so give them some simple guidance—training, if you will—on using it appropriately, skillfully, and positively. What should you teach them? Why, how to WIN, of course!

W—WWGT = WHAT WOULD YOUR GRANDMOTHER THINK?

This is a safe and easily understood way to judge a post's appropriateness. Tell your athletes that if their grandmother would think that what they are about to post is bad, then they shouldn't post it. If their grandmother would be proud, go with it. If their grandmother wouldn't understand it? Well, then maybe they need to make their post a bit more clear.

I—INTENTIONAL

Remind your athletes that everything they do, they should do with intention. What does that mean? Simply put, they shouldn't just throw stuff out there on their social media. Rather, when they post, they should really be thinking about what they are saying. They should deeply consider what exactly they are writing and how other people may view it. They should analyze each word, picture, or video; try to put themselves in the shoes of a social media user; and figure out what the post might mean or represent to someone who doesn't share their background or experiences. Every word your athletes put down, every picture or video they are thinking of posting, should have a purpose. They shouldn't post just to post. They should be able to truthfully say, "I know what I am posting here, there's a reason to post it, and this will not hurt my future."

N—NOW

The last part of WIN is *now*. That is, after your athletes consider whether their post is going to be in the best interest of themselves, the team, the school, and their family and confirm that they are being absolutely intentional about every word or picture they are about to post, they need to ask themselves, "Is now the time to post it?" Maybe it meets all the criteria—it's good, it's cool, it's safe. Grandma would approve and the intention behind the post is acceptable. If that is the case, then no worries, right? They can push the button with a clear conscience. Not quite: maybe now is not the time. Maybe they need to rethink what they're doing. Maybe their post is something to save for later. Maybe it would be better at a different time. Impress up on them that they need to make sure that they always know when their best time to post, their post's now, is. Moments move fast; they need to know that it is okay if their now comes later. The reason why later may be better is simply because any amount of time allows them to rethink their posts and get their emotions closer to neutral, where they can make a more logical and better decision about posting.

The take a time-out and WIN strategy may sound a bit simplistic, maybe even ridiculous, to you as a coach and even to your athletes. However, people have a tendency to remember mnemonic devices, especially when they come in the form of simple, silly sayings. If you can get your athletes to take the time-out and WIN, you will eliminate a ton of future problems. If your athletes remember even just the W out of the WIN acronym, you will avoid a significant amount of drama.

12

SOCIAL MEDIA BRANDING BENEFITS AND OTHER FINAL THOUGHTS

If I show you a Nike Swoosh without the word *Nike*, you still know what that is. That is amazing branding. When a logo is so powerful we automatically identify and respond to it, especially in a positive way, it demonstrates the power of the brand. Many of you are at smaller colleges and universities with brands that are not especially well-known. For you, using social media in the right way can be a game changer in helping you grow your brand. Others of you work for athletic departments and universities with brands so large that expanding the brand's reach and recognition is not an immediate concern. If a well-known university decides to not be a part of the social media game, that decision may not hurt it initially as long as the school's teams are winning championships. However, universities that do embrace social media and use it interactively will increase their brand recognition among millennials. Social media word of mouth is huge among millennials, and if they see you as an active part of their world, your brand will have more value than that of any university or college that does not make the effort to get on millennials' radar.

Coaches, I want to talk to you about your personal social media brand. Most coaches today see the value in it. However, there are still those who express skepticism. That is fine, and I do not want to try to force anyone who does not want to use social media to use it, because such a disinterested person would probably not take the time to truly understand it and may inadvertently use it poorly. After all, the safest play is to not use social media at all. However, as I have repeatedly stated, with the NCAA rule change, coaches can now put themselves in front of recruits they have never had an opportunity to recruit before simply by being active on social media. Coaches and administrators who believe that social media doesn't make an impact are thinking in old school terms, from a time when a school's name was enough to attract a prospect. Although that was once was the case, such effortless recruiting is no longer so common. Recruited players have already left Division 1 programs on the basis of a series of tweets. How many future recruits do you believe will change schools if they see a coach like, favorite, retweet, or tag their posts? Keep watching, because I predict the number will be far larger than you imagine.

You, as a coach, have a tremendous opportunity to ramp up the effectiveness of your recruiting by expanding your brand into the social media world. Your activity, interaction, and engagement with young people through social media will make an impression on these kids, because you, the coach, are paying attention to them. The bigger your social media brand, the bigger your impact on this rising generation. The strategy may sound too simple to work, but remember that young people today are swayed by the attention they receive. You now have access to their world. Be a part of it, influence it, and make a positive impression that demonstrates you are a participant in it. This is a tremendous opportunity for you to attract the athletes you want to your program.

Keep in mind, though, that the young people you are recruiting are the natives of these platforms. Chances are you are the immigrant. Therefore, they pay very close attention to what you do when you use social media. What are they looking for? Authenticity. These young people can read very quickly whether you are trying to get their attention just because you want something from them (like their athletic skills) or if you are being authentic in your interaction. They want to be seen as people first—as individuals with talent—and not simply as commodities that fill slots on a roster. This is why you cannot use social media only as a recruiting tool. You have to be part of the social media world. It is not enough to get in touch with the people you want to recruit. You need to be able to speak the different languages of the social media platforms and demonstrate that you understand the unwritten rules, norms, and expectations of these worlds. These young people want to see that you are a willing, active participant on the social media platforms they use rather than simply an awkward stranger hanging out in cyberspace in the hopes of recruiting them. In another words, you better have something to post that does not have to do with recruiting.

FINAL THOUGHTS

There is much, much more that can be said about social media. However, what I have attempted to do here is give you a brief primer on social media, some food for thought, and practical suggestions for how to handle social media, both on your own part and that of your athletes. I have also written a book for your student athletes, titled *The Social Media Playbook for Student Athletes*, that gives them some similar things to think about when using social media. Most social media training for athletes focuses so much on the negatives that after a while, the student athlete tunes out. This doesn't mean that we should not explain the possible pitfalls to them, but that cannot be the only thing we talk about. We need to give them practical, positive examples.

Social media is not a fad, and it is not going away. This new method of communication is part of everyday life. Does it come with problems? Yes, but it is here to stay, so it is up to us to adjust to the new reality.

Social media is a powerful tool. It is neither good nor bad; it is how people use it that determines its value. Many a business and many a person have become incredibly successful as a result of social media. People pursue jobs through different social media channels and have built careers based entirely on social media. Social media offers far more positives than negatives. It is not the platform's fault when things go wrong. Lack of understanding, lack of self-control, and peer pressure are the reasons for social media problems.

As a coach and an administrator, you may try to ensure that your athletes and your staff do not misuse social media. Make sure that you have a plan, establish goals like you would for your sport, and be more proactive than reactive. Monitoring is not enough. You should have rules, and those rules must have consequences if they are broken. Whatever you choose to do, those rules and their consequences must be consistently applied, and make sure you do not punish others for what one person has done. Anticipate the negative fallout a social media misstep will generate.

Use social media as a branding tool, and make sure it is also part of your recruiting strategy. This generation of student athletes as well as future generations of student athletes are increasingly paying attention to what you do on social media. If you choose not to be a part of social media, do not become upset if an athlete you recruited decommits and goes to what you believe is a less prestigious program because that program used social media to lure the athlete away.

This also means that you and your staff have to do the right things on social media. It sounds absurd to suggest that coaches can do the wrong thing on social media, but coaches without the appropriate social media training can fall into the same social media traps as their student athletes do. You and your staff need policies and a social media strategy that are appropriate and fit within the rules of the NCAA, NAIA, or your conference.

You have a tremendous amount of responsibility on your plate. Social media is likely the last thing you want to add to your already extensive purview. However, it cannot be avoided or ignored. You can only do your best to control it, and that is not going to be an easy task. The young people in your athletic program need help to understand that they are living in era when everything they say and do is going to be scrutinized. Further, after their college athletic career, they will undertake a professional career, and it is likely that their social media use will have an effect, positive or negative, on their job prospects as well as other aspects of their future. We can either help them navigate social media well so that they have as many opportunities as possible or ignore it and hope nothing happens. Let's be proactive and give them skills. Being proactive is not going to solve all of the problems that social media may bring, but it will certainly help limit them.

I have great respect for what you do. Having been around and working in athletic programs, I know it is not the easy, game-playing life some people believe it to be. However, I also know that in these programs, I have encountered some of the most competitive, strongest, smartest people with great integrity that I have ever met. They love their athletes, as I am sure you also do. Realize that you have a tremendous influence on the kids in your program. College athletics is about more than just playing a sport: it is about life. You help your athletes grow into the women or men they eventually become. Stay the course and continue to be the person to whom your athletes can turn for guidance on any topic. Social media may be a new characteristic of college athletics, a complication that you feel you and your program don't currently need. However, as you learn and grow in your understanding of social media, you can help the young people in your athletic program more than you can even imagine.

Stay successful!
Jay Izso, the Internet Doctor

NOTES

1. Kevin DeShazo, "Social Media Use of Student Athletes: 2016 Survey Results," *Fieldhouse Media*, April 13, 2016, http://www.fieldhousemedia.net/social-media-use-of-student-athletes-2016-survey-results/.
2. Ibid.
3. "New NCAA Social Media Policy Begins Today," *ESPN San Antonio*, August 1, 2016, http://www.espnsa.com/new-ncaa-social-media-policy-begins-today/.
4. Ibid.
5. "Football: Pollard Apologizes for 'Three Amigos' Cinco de Mayo Social Media Post," *Ames Tribune*, May 6, 2016, http://www.amestrib.com/sports/football-pollard-apologizes-three-amigos-cinco-de-mayo-social-media-post.

SOCIAL MEDIA PLAYBOOK HIGHLIGHTS

Social media is defined as any online platform where people can post words, pictures, or videos that have the potential to be viewed by anyone in real time. The main ones you need to know (and the things typically posted there are the following):

- ► Facebook (words, pictures, videos, live streaming)
- ► Twitter (words, pictures, videos)
- ► Snapchat (pictures and videos)
- ► Instagram (pictures and videos)

What is posted on any of these platforms can never truly be deleted, even if you take it down after posting. NOTHING DIES ON THE INTERNET. Therefore, it is absolutely essential that the content and implications of anything posted be known, considered, and intentionally shared. Remember, "freedom of speech" is not "freedom from consequences." There is no such thing as freedom from consequences, which can be immediate and harsh (think lost scholarships) as well as long-ranging (think future jobs).

You're a step ahead if you know the 6 Myths of Social Media:

- ▶ Myth 1: Student athletes can say what they want because they are young.
- ▶ Myth 2: People only care about Division 1 athletes and coaches; they don't care about Division 2, Division 3, or smaller schools.
- ▶ Myth 3: No one cares about sports other than football and basketball when it comes to social media.
- ▶ Myth 4: If I tell people that my account was hacked or say, "I was taken out of context," people will leave it alone.
- ▶ Myth 5: Social media is my business, not yours.
- ▶ Myth 6: I have freedom of speech, so I can say and do what I want.

When talking to your athletes about social media, make sure they know:

It is safer for your athlete to just assume that his or her private life is over once he or she starts using social media.

People will forget all the good that they do, but people will be quick to remember nearly all of their past transgressions.

You have rules about social media. Be clear on what rules you will enforce, how you are going to enforce them, and what consequences are going to be associated with inappropriate social media use.

It is important to continually educate and remind athletes how to use social media correctly and responsibly to avoid problems in the first place. There are some strategies they can use to help post positive, career-enhancing social media content to build their brands and to play defensively in situations that are inherently dangerous online.

Offensive social media plays:

► Volunteer play
► Travel play
► Selfie wefie strategy
► Documentary play
► Practice drills
► Dancing coaches

Defensive social media plays:

► Game loss zone defense
► Corner blitz
► Team defense
► Deactivation defense

Posting strategy: Take a time-out and go for the WIN
    Time-Out: Pause 30 seconds before posting, then WIN:

        W—WWGT = What Would Your Grandmother
                        Think?
        I—Intentional
        N–Now

ABOUT THE AUTHOR

JAY IZSO, the Internet Doctor ®, is a multi-award winning author, professional speaker, podcaster, and business/life coach. He works with entrepreneurs, professional associations, colleges and universities, and businesses of all sizes. Jay empowers his audiences to recognize the psychological needs of their clientele and imparts the tools and knowledge to build relationships and garner loyalty.

Having literally written the book on the subject, *Got Social Mediology? Using Psychology to Master Social Media for Your Business without Spending a Dime*, Jay Izso is a pioneer in the field.

Jay's upcoming three new titles to be released fall of 2018 include: *The Social Media Playbook for Student Athletes*; *The Social Media Playbook for Coaches & Administrators*; and *Lessons from the Farm: Essential Rules for Success*

Jay enjoys working with and motivating audiences all over the world. When he's not busy writing, speaking, and coaching, Jay enjoys life as a part-time beach freak, musician, sports fan, and classic movie buff. He lives in Raleigh, North Carolina, with his wife, Linda Craft, and their dog, Bandit.

Organizations and Memberships:
- National Speakers Association—Professional Member
- American Psychological Association

For more information about, his books,
or to book him for an event, visit:

www.jayizso.com